WOMEN OF THE SPIRIT BIBLE STUDY

Vol. V: Women of Compassion

JOY HANEY

All Scripture quotations are from the King James Version of the Holy Bible unless otherwise noted.

Women of the Spirit Bible Studies by Joy Haney
Published by Radiant Life Publications
Stockton, California
First Printing
Copyright @ August 1995

Printed in the United States of America.

Library of Congress Catalog Number 94-68446
ISBN 1-880969-21-1

Women of the Spirit Bible Studies

The *Women of the Spirit Bible Studies* are designed for women who desire to walk in the Spirit as stated in Galatians 5:16, 25. "This I say then, Walk in the Spirit, and ye shall not fulfill the lust of the flesh. If we live in the Spirit, let us also walk in the Spirit."

People sense there is something happening in the world that is different, and at times frightening. These are days of destiny. In the church world there is an urgency that has gripped the hearts of Christians everywhere. Revival is exploding in many countries, and a spirit of evangelism is increasing. This is the day to become a woman of compassion, reaching out to a world that is hungry to hear more about Jesus Christ.

Volume V has been added to this group of Bible Studies for women, as the Spirit has directed. My prayer is that your eyes will be opened to what *you* as an individual can do for Jesus right where you live. May the holy presence of God dwell richly in your heart and home as you stretch forth your hand to the needy. May His face shine upon you, and may the blessing of the Lord be rich in your life as you do His bidding.

Women of the Spirit Bible Study

Vol. V: Women of Compassion

Table of Contents

Lessons:

Women of the Spirit Bible Study

Compassion

Lesson I

I.   COMPASSION

A. What is Compassion?

    1. Webster's Definitions:

        a. Sympathetic to the distress or misfortunes of others to the point of action.

        b. It is to be responsive and tender.

    2. Roget's Thesaurus gives the following synonyms for compassion.

        a. sympathy
        b. tenderness
        c. kindness
        d. mercy
        e. heart

    3. "The dew of compassion is a tear."
                        Lord Bryon

B. Why is compassion important?

    1. It is important because Jesus emphasized it.

a. The story in Mark 5:1-19 is a story of terror, passion, hopelessness, demon possession and deliverance. When Jesus came into the country of the Gadarenas he was met by a man with an unclean spirit, who was crying, wandering in the mountains, and cutting himself with stones. Jesus immediately commanded the unclean spirits to come out of him.

b. Notice, what Jesus emphasized after the man was delivered.

    i. Mark 5:19 says, "Howbeit Jesus suffered him not, but saith unto him, Go home to thy friends, and tell them how great things the Lord hath done for thee, and hath had compassion on thee."

    ii. The two things that Jesus wanted talked about were **the great things the Lord had done** and **the compassion Jesus had shown**.

    iii. Jesus had a reason for emphasizing compassion. He knew that this story would be read by many people, and He wanted to underscore the importance of this quality.

2. It is important because no one can be a true Christian who does not exercise love and compassion toward others.

a. I John 4:20 says, "If a man say, I love God, and hateth his brother, he is a liar: for he that loveth not his brother whom he hath seen, how can he love God whom he hath not seen?"

b. I John 4:8 says, "He that loveth not knoweth not God; for God is love."

C. Compassion is synonymous with God.

    1. Psalm 78:38 says, "But he, being full of compassion, forgave their iniquity, and destroyed them not."

        a. God was *full* of compassion.

        b. Compassion is not always deserved.

    2. Psalm 86:15 says, "But thou, O Lord, art a God full of compassion and gracious, long suffering, and plenteous in mercy and truth."

    3. Psalms 145:8 says, "The Lord is gracious, and full of compassion; slow to anger and of great mercy."

D. Compassion means letting the others know you care, and being a friend to those in need.

    1. An eminent clergyman sat in his study, busily engaged in preparing his Sunday sermon, when his little boy toddled into the room, held up his pinched finger, and said with an expression of suffering, "Look, pa, how I hurt it." The father, interrupted in the middle of a sentence, glanced hastily at him, and with the slightest tone of impatience said, "I can't help it, sonny." The little fellow's eyes grew bigger, and as he turned to go out, he said in a low voice, "Yes, you could; you might have said 'Oh'!"

    2. The North American Indians' word for "friend" was, "one-who-carries-my-sorrows-on-his-back." This shows compassion.

    3. An English publication offered a prize for the best definition of "friend," and among the thousands of answers received were the following:

        a. One who multiplies joys, divides grief.

b.   A volume of sympathy poured in cloth.

c.   Here is the one that won the prize: A friend is the one who comes in when the whole world has gone out.

4.   "One thing more I ask"
Dear God, another day is done
And I have seen the golden sun
Swing in the arch from east to west
And sink behind the pines to rest.
I thank Thee that Thou gavest me
The power of sight that I may see
The tinted glories of Thy skies,
An earthly glimpse of Paradise:
The power to hear the evening breeze
Swelling in organ harmonies;
The power to feel the tender grasp
Of loving hands in friendship's clasp;
I thank Thee for these gifts to me;
But one thing more I ask of Thee:
From out Thy bounteous, gracious hand
Give me the power to understand,
To understand--to sympathize
To note the pain in others' eyes;
To have the power rightly to read
The kindly motive of each deed.
And this I humbly ask of Thee
Because I know Thou lovest me.
                                  Author unknown

E.   Compassion is a heart-throb on fire with love.

1.   "We live in deeds, not years; in thought, not breaths; in feelings, not in figures on a dial. We should count time by heart-throbs. He most lives who thinks most, feels the noblest, acts the best."
                                  Philip James Bailey

2. We are commanded to have a heart totally given to love. Mark 12:30-31 says, "And thou shalt love the Lord thy God with all thy heart, and with all thy soul, and with all thy mind, and with all thy strength: this is the first commandment. And the second is like, namely this, Thou shalt love thy neighbor as thyself." This is a very passionate love that will result in compassion.

3. Jesus had a heart that throbbed with compassion. According to Matthew 20:34, when two blind men cried out to Him so that they might receive their sight, "Jesus had compassion on them, and touched their eyes: and immediately their eyes received sight."

   a. Compassion always tries to meet needs.

   b. Compassion produces actions.

   c. Compassion makes a difference in the life of another.

Lesson I Quiz

1. Give the definition of compassion.

2. Why is compassion important?

3. What does compassion do?

   a.

   b.

   c.

4. What did Jesus emphasize to the man of the Gadarenes, after he delivered him of the unclean spirit?

5. Give Scriptures that deal with compassion.

   a.

   b.

   c.

6. Give the quote by Philip James Bailey.

Women of the Spirit Bible Study

Women With
A Mission

Lesson II

II. WOMEN WITH A MISSION

A. Every woman is important, and compassion for others will help her find true purpose in life.

   1. No woman is useless. She may feel as if she is, but that is the way the devil wants her to feel. Every women should be on fire with a mission. The Bible is filled with women who cared enough about others and God's kingdom to do something. Look at the following women who are our examples.

      a. *Jochebed*: Exodus 2:1-11; 6:20; Numbers 26:59; Hebrews 11:23.
      She changed the tide of history by having the courage to stand against the king's decree. From her Godly motherhood came the following three great leaders:

         i. Moses, who became one of the greatest national leaders and legislators the world has ever known.

         ii. Aaron, who became Israel's first high priest.

iii.   Miriam, who was the gifted poet and
         musician.

b.   *Hannah*: I Samuel 1; 2:1,21.
       She gave the world Samuel who became Prophet
       and Judge of Israel. She prayed him into existence.

c.   *Jehosheba*: II Kings 11:2; II Chronicles 22:11.
       She saved Joash, the royal seed, from the
       murderous plot of the wicked woman, Athaliah,
       who wanted to be queen.

d.   *Deborah*: Judges 4 -5; Hebrews 11:32-34.
       She became a Prophetess and Judge of Israel. At a
       time of despair she aroused the nation from its
       lethargy. Then she went with Barak as a warrior
       against Sisera.

e.   *Esther*: Esther 4.
       She saved the whole Jewish nation from death and
       destruction.

f.   *Mary*: Matthew 1-2; 12:46; Luke 1-2; John 2:1-
       11; 19:25.
       She became the vessel that brought Jesus to the
       world.

g.   *Dorcas*: Acts 9:36-43.
       The Scripture calls her a "certain disciple." She
       was a Christian who sewed many garments for
       other Christians, and was so loved that when she
       died many grieved her death. The Scripture says
       about her. "This women was full of good works
       and almsdeeds which she did" (Acts 9:36).
       Among her good works was that of fashioning
       coats and garments for widows and the needy of
       her church and community.

h. *Huldah*: II Kings 22:14-20; II Chronicles 34:22-33.
She was a prophetess who could be found sitting in the central part of the city ready to receive and counsel any who wished to inquire of Jehovah. She unveiled the future of a nation when Hlkiah the priest found the book in the temple. Josiah immediately sent for Huldah. Her prophetic message and the public reading of the law brought about a revival.

i. *Lydia*: Acts 16:12-15, 40; Philippians 1:1-10.
She was a business woman who was known for her Christian hospitality and open house. She was a devout woman.

2. Any woman who helps another will be blessed by God, and others will be glad she lived.

a. "So long as we love, we serve. So long as we are loved by others I would almost say we are indispensable; and no [woman] is useless while [she] has a friend."
Robert Louis Stevensen

b. "Blessed is he that considereth the poor: the Lord will deliver him in time of trouble. the Lord will preserve him, and keep him alive; and he shall be blessed upon the earth" (Psalm 41:1-2).
The poor can be anyone who has a need, whether it be financial, spiritual, physical, or emotional.

B. Women with a mission have many fine character traits. Three important ones are the following:

1. Submission: They obeyed what God put in their heart.

a. When Mary was told she would be the mother of the Messiah, she said "Behold the handmaid of the Lord, be it unto me according to thy word" (Luke 1:38).

b. When Esther was told that she had come to the kingdom for such a time as this, she said, "and so will I go in unto the king; which is not according to the law: and if I perish, I perish" (Esther 4:16).

2. Devotion: They had a desire to know God, and prayer to him was a part of their lifestyle.

a. Hannah: The Scriptures says, "And Hannah prayed" (I Samuel 2:1).

b. Lydia: The Scripture says, "she worshipped God" (Acts 16:14).

c. Mary: Luke 1:28 says, "The Lord is with thee: Blessed art thou among women." Luke 1:46 says, "And Mary said, my soul doth magnify the Lord."

3. Courage: Although often afraid, they accomplished their work with bravery and determination.

a. Deborah led the armies of the children of Israel to victory.
"And Barak said unto her, If thou wilt go with me, then I will go: but if thou wilt not go with me, then I will not go" (Judges 4:8). She went.

b. Esther was afraid and did not want to do what she had been asked to do because it could mean her death, but she did it anyway saying, "If I perish, I perish" (Esther 4:16).

c.   Jochabed disobeyed a wicked king's command, that could have meant death to her. "And Pharaoh charged all his people, saying, Every son that is born ye shall cast into the river" (Exodus 1:22). She saved Moses from death in spite of the threat to her life.

C.   Women with a mission are alive and vibrant and live meaningful lives.

    1.   Seemingly insignificant women take on a new glow of radiance when they become women with a mission. This is exemplified by the following story about a jewel:

    "A gentleman once visited a great jewelry store, owned by a friend. His friend showed him magnificent diamonds, and other splendid stones. Amongst these stones his eye lighted on one that seemed quite lustreless, and, pointing to it, he said: "That has no beauty at all." But his friend put it in the hollow of his hand, and shut his hand, and then in a few moments opened it again.

    "What a surprise! The entire stone gleamed with all the splendors of the rainbow. 'What have you done to it?' asked the astonished gazer. His friend answered: 'This is an opal. It is what we call the sympathetic jewel. It only needs to be gripped with the human hand to bring out its wonderful beauty."

Author unknown

When a woman grips another human hand and helps bring them to Christ, she too glows with new beauty and purpose. As she is held in the hollow of the Master's hand, she in turn will fulfill His mission, which is to save the world. It is when a woman touches Christ that she can then touch others, and she will be made beautiful.

    2.   Their minds are turned outward instead of always reflecting on self.

a. "A person completely wrapped up in himself makes a small package.... The great day comes when a man begins to get himself off his hands. He has lived, let us say, in a mind like a room surrounded by mirrors. Every way he turned he saw himself. Now, however, some of the mirrors change to windows. He can see through them to objective outlooks that challenge his interests. He begins to get out of himself-no longer the prisoner of self-reflections but a free man in a world where persons, causes, truths, and values exist, worthful for their own sakes. Thus to pass from a mirror-mind to a mind with windows is an essential element in the development of a real personality. Without that experience no one ever achieves a meaningful life."
Harry Emerson Fosdick

b. "If I can stop one heart from breaking,
I shall not live in vain;
If I can ease one life the aching,
Or cool one pain,
Or help one fainting robin
Unto his nest again,
I shall not live in vain."
Emily Dickinson

3. Mary must have been glowing when she walked into the house of Zacharias and Elisabeth, for when Elisabeth heard Mary's greeting Elisabeth was filled with the Holy Ghost, and she said the baby leaped within her womb. Mary answered her out of the vibrant fullness of her heart. "My soul doth magnify the LORD. And my Spirit hath rejoiced in God my Saviour" (Luke 1:46-47). She was a woman with a mission.

D.   Our mission is to stand in Christ's stead.

1.   The following poem says it well:

"Christ Has No Hands"
Christ has no hands but our hands to do His work today
He has no feet but our feet to lead men in the way
He has no tongue but our tongue to tell men how He died
He has no help but our help to bring them to His side.
We are the only Bible the careless world will read
We are the sinner's gospel; we are the scoffer's creed
We are the Lord's last message, given in word and deed;
What if the type is crooked? What if the print is blurred?
What if our hands are busy with other work than His?
What if our feet are walking where sin's allurement is?
What if our tongue is speaking of things His lips would spurn?
How can we hope to help Him or welcome His return?
Annie Johnston Flint

2.   "During [the] war, a church in Strasbourg was destroyed. Nothing remained except a heap of rubble and broken glass, or so the people thought till they began clearing away the masonry. Then they found a statue of Christ still standing erect. In spite of all the bombing it was unharmed except that both hands were missing. Eventually rebuilding of the church began.
One day a sculptor saw the figure of Christ, and offered to carve new hands. The church officials met to consider the sculptor's friendly gesture- and decided not to accept the offer. Why? because the members of that church said: "Our broken statue touches the spirits of men, but that He has no hands to minister to the needy of feed the hungry or enrich the poor- except our hands. He inspires. We perform."
Author unknown

3. Matthew 25:40 says, "Inasmuch as ye have done it unto one of the least of these my brethren, ye have done it unto me." Jesus was referring to Matthew 25:35, "For I was an hungered, and ye gave me meat; I was thirsty, and ye gave me drink; I was a stranger, and ye took me in."

4. Someone once said the following:
    "A Christian is a mind through which Christ thinks.
    A heart through which Christ speaks;
    A voice through which Christ speaks;
    A hand through which Christ helps."

Lesson II Quiz

1.　Name nine women who did what God put in their heart to do. Please, tell what they did and give Scripture references.

    a.

    b.

    c.

    d.

    e.

    f.

    g.

    h.

    i.

2.　List three important character traits of these women.

    a.
    b.
    c.

Lesson III

III. WOMEN OF EVANGELISM

A. Every woman should be an evangelist.

    1. The greatest message Jesus instructed to mankind, (the message of the resurrection), was first delivered by a woman. Jesus said to Mary *go and tell*.

        a. John 20:16-18 says, "Jesus saith unto her, Mary. She turned herself, and saith unto him, Rabboni; which is to say Master.
Jesus saith unto her... go to my brethren, and say unto them, I ascend unto my Father.... Mary Magdalene came and told the disciples."

        b. Matthew 28:10 says, "Go tell my brethren".

    2. When Jesus spoke to the woman of Samaria by Jacob's well, and told her all about herself, she became an evangelist.

        a. John 4:28-30 says, "The women then left her waterpot, and went her way into the city, and saith to the men, Come, see a man, which told me all things that ever I did: is not this the Christ?"

b. What were the results of her witness? John 4:30 says, "Then they went out of the city, and came unto him."

3. An evangelist does not necessarily mean a traveling preacher. The definition we will lift out of Webster's Dictionary is *an evangelizer*.

a. What is an Evangelizer? It is anyone who is instrumental in converting someone to Jesus.

b. This means that you as a woman can convert others to Jesus, and as He sent Mary to *go and tell*, He is sending you. What are some of the ways you can do this?

i. You can use unstructured witnessing.

- Witness to others while going about your business.

ii. You can use structured witnessing.

- Set a time to teach someone a Home Bible Study.

- Hand out tracks (keep them in your purse).

- Telephone witnessing

- Teach your children daily from the Bible.

c. Remember that Jesus evangelized on the shores of Galilee, in the open fields, sitting on a rock in the mountains, or while in homes.

d.   A spirit of evangelism must grip the church, and *women* are the best evangelizers there are. Witnessing for Jesus must become a lifestyle.

4.   When women get so in love with Jesus, and get out of themselves, something wonderful happens.

a.   In the book, *Man with a Destiny: Bill Drost The Pentecost*, Mike and Lorna Wieteska share a moving story about an experience of a 17 year old girl who received the gift of the Holy Ghost. She went to Brother & Sister Drost and told them that she wanted to go tell her people about Jesus. Brother Drost said later about her, "She was so without physical strength...not much more than a girl...yet in the Spirit she was resolute, undauntable, powerful...completely unaware of her Joan of Arc aura." So up the mountain to LaMorena, Columbia, she went, praying persistently that God would help her speak to the people. Many recognized and greeted her as she made her way through the banana and coffee plantations. Everyone she saw she invited to come to a meeting she planned to hold in her parents' house. She had an uncle named Saul who owned the only saloon on the mountain. He was in the Last Chance Saloon that particular night and since nobody was coming, he thought there might be an insurrection taking place. Suddenly he heard the sound of hooves outside, and ran outside shouting to the rider on the horse, "Hey, what's going on, where is everybody tonight?"
"Oh, haven't you heard? Everybody's at the gospel meeting that girl is holding!"
When Saul heard that his cousin, Eucaris, had found religion, he was furious. He jumped on his horse and made his way quickly to the meeting, and planned to break it up. Approaching the house he saw many animals tied outside in the moonlight. Glancing through the window, he saw his cousin

praying with people who were kneeling down. Pulling himself up to his full height and throwing his chest out, he barged through the door with his shoulder, making a dramatic entrance, with his hands on pistols.   But that was as far as he got.

"Eucaris had never felt such a spirit of evangelism. She recited all she had seen happen in Cali, and preached a down-to-earth message on the love of God and the need to repent. After her telling simple stories, the folks came under tremendous conviction, and some were weeping, many getting right with God. Eucaris wept with them, praying earnestly for God to baptize them with His Spirit.

"At that moment cousin Saul came in with a bang. Looking up startled, Eucaris took in the situation and prayed that God would stop Saul from ruining the meeting. Saul couldn't move. He stood transfixed at the door, dazed and confused. It was like in a dream; nothing would move, not an arm, not a finger not an eyelid. He could have been enclosed in warm, transparent steel. People in the room continued kneeling in prayer. Suddenly, in the atmosphere, he felt tremendously unclean: his cousin came toward him in seemingly slow motion; she looked radiantly beautiful, and she looked...*clean*. The dark eyes of Eucaris looked at him from unplumbed depths, with a tenderness he had never seen the like of. It was as though some other force was in those eyes. Saul wilted as he looked into them. She put her hands on his head and he felt fire go through him as she said, 'You need Jesus.'

"At that moment, released from the force that held him, he dropped to his knees. He could do no more. All he wanted to do was cry and confess and be free from the horror of his condition, and to find the beauty he perceived about him. Saul stayed there a long time. When he did get up, the first thing he did was to go back to his bar and pour all his liquor down the mountainside. He was through with it. Forever."

All because one 17 year old girl had compassion on her people, and cared enough to go and tell.

b.   In the book, *Revivals,* Fischer shares the following story.

"A poor uncultured and untaught Kaffir woman on hearing of the love of Jesus gladly received the truth, and as the Holy Spirit took up His abode in her heart, she felt the yearning to go out to the thousands of her people lying in sin and darkness all about her. She had no education, no command of language to impart the blessed truth that had come into her life, no way of travel, and no money to assist her; but she took the little gospel leaflet or tract that had been given to her by the traveling missionary and started out on foot to spread the gospel light. She would enter a village, go directly to the chief, and silently hand him the tract written in his own dialect.

"He would read it, then looking at her full in the eye, demand to know about this Jesus. She would then tell in simple words of what had taken place in her heart. Other leaders would be called, the paper read and re-read, more questions asked, and the power of God would take hold of the people. She simply waited for God to work. She had no thought nor concern about her own efforts. Her confidence was in the power that had taken hold of her darkened heart and transformed it. When she saw the tears falling, heard the cries of joy about her, she knew the light had come. She would then take her tract and steal away into another village. This was repeated again and again until the light broke into all the country for miles."

B.   Evangelism was the passion of the heart of Jesus.

1.   John 4:35 shows the urgency that He felt. "Say not ye, There are yet four months, and then cometh harvest? behold I say unto you, lift up your eyes, and look in the fields; for they are white already to harvest."

2.   Jesus felt the deep needs of the people, and did everything He could to help them, but He realized that many more people needed to get involved. See the scenario of His heart in Matthew 9:35-38.

a.   Verse 35 says, "And Jesus went about all the cities and villages, teaching in their synagogues, and preaching the gospel of the kingdom, and healing every sickness and every disease among the people."

b.   Verse 36 says, "But when he saw the multitudes, he was moved with compassion on them, because they fainted, and were scattered abroad, as sheep having no shepherd."

c.   Verse 37 says, "Pray ye therefore the Lord of the harvest, that he will send forth laborers into his harvest."

3.   Will you help answer that prayer request?
       Oh, yes, you will still wash the dishes, sweep the floor, cook those meals, and some of you will go to work, but a new urgency and a spirit of evangelism will take hold of you. No longer will you be depressed over what has been, or what could be, but you will be on fire with a passion to reach the lost, or to help others know Jesus more intimately.
       It could be over the backyard fence, at lunch on the job, maybe standing in a line at a grocery store, or sitting on a couch with a Bible open on your lap.

You do not have to be behind a pulpit to evangelize. You are the only Jesus that some people will ever see. Represent Him well!

4. Someone once said, "Jesus' trained ears could hear a beggar's cry above the shouts of the throng." Pray for this kind of hearing today.

5. The story is told of William Booth's response to King Edward.
    When the king asked Booth to write in his autograph album, he bent forward, took the pen, and wrote the following:
    Your Majesty,
    Some men's ambition is art.
    Some men's ambition is fame
    Some men's ambition is gold,
    My ambition is the souls of men.

6. This should be the ambition of every woman, who has received Truth. When we receive the Holy Spirit of God, we become His ambassadors (II Corinthians 5:20). No longer do we exist as we once were, but we are made new. II Corinthians 5:17 says, "Therefore if any man be in Christ, he is a new creature: old things are passed away; behold, all things are become new."
    I Corinthians 6:19-20 says, "ye are not your own for, ye are bought with a price."

C. Jesus did not live in a palace surrounded by guards: He touched the people.

1. Mark 1: 40-41 says, "And there came a leper to him, beseeching him, and kneeling down to him, and saying unto him, if thou wilt, thou canst make me clean. And Jesus moved with compassion, put forth his hand, and *touched* him, and saith unto him, I will, be thou clean."

2.   When Jesus saw the widow in the city of Nain, walking beside her only son who was being carried out dead, his heart was touched. Luke 7:13-14 says, "And when the Lord saw her, he had compassion on her, and said unto her, weep not. And *he came and touched* the bier: and they that bare him stood still. And he said, Young man, I say unto thee, Arise."

    a.   This should be the propelling force of each woman's life: to *lift* people up.

    b.   As Jesus touched people, so should we touch them with the gospel and with Love.

3.   The virtuous women touched people. Proverbs 31:20 says, "She stretcheth out her hand to the poor; yea, she reacheth forth her hands to the needy." Hands are used for touching.

4.   It is impossible to please God without touching or helping lift people out of their despair. I John 3:17 says, "But whoso hath this world's good, and seeth his brother have need, and shutteth up his bowels of compassion from him, how dwelleth the love of God in him?"

    a.   The following are translations of I John 3:17:

        i.   *"Steels his heart against him"*
            The Twentieth Century New Testament

        ii.   *"Closes his heart against him"*
            Richard Francis Weymouth

    b.   "Let Me Be Aware"
        God--let me be aware.
        Let me not stumble blindly down life's ways,
        Just seeking somehow safely to get through
        the days,
        Hand never groping for another hand,

Not even groping for another hand,
Not even wondering why it all was planned,
Eyes to the ground, unseeking for the light,
Soul never longing for a wild wing flight,
Please, keep me eager just to do my share.
God--let me be aware.

God--let me be aware.
Stab my soul fiercely with others' pain,
Let me walk seeing horror and stain.
Let my hand, groping, find other hands.
Give me the heart that divines, understands.
Give me the courage, wounded, to fight.
Fill me with knowledge and drench me with light.
Please--keep me eager just to do my share.
God--let me be aware.

Miriam Teichner

5.   It is imperative for the church to become more aware of
     other people's needs, and not close itself up in its own
     world.

a.   "If I Had Known"
          If I had known what trouble you were bearing;
          What griefs were in the silence of your face;
          I would have been more gentle, and more caring
          And tried to give you gladness for a space.
          I would have brought more warmth into the place,
               If I had known.
          If I had known what thoughts despairing drew you;
          (Why do we never try to understand?)
          I would have lent a little friendship to you,
          And slipped my hand within your hand,
          And made your stay more pleasant in the land,
               If I had known.

Mary Carolyn Davies

b.   Let me not shut myself within myself
Nor dedicate my days to petty things,
Let there be many windows in my life,
The entrance to my heart a door that swings.
Save me from self-preferment that would gain
Its cloistered place, safe sheltered from the strife.
But purposeful and calm and sweet and sane,
Lord, keep me in the Living Room of life.
Author unknown

Lesson III Quiz

1.　What did Jesus instruct Mary to go and tell the disciples?

2.　What is an evangelizer?

3.　Give examples of structured and unstructured witnessing, and how a woman can be an evangelizer.

　　a.

　　b.

　　c.

　　d.

　　e.

4.　What should be the propelling force of each woman's life?

5.　Quote Proverbs 31:20.

6.　Quote I John 3:17.

7.　What was the prayer request and scenario of the heart of Jesus found in Matthew 9:35-38?

IV. WOMEN OF SACRIFICE

A. When Jesus saw a need, He always served it.

    1. Mark 6:34 says, "And when Jesus, when he came out, *saw* much people, and was moved with compassion toward them."

        a. What was the result of this compassion? First, He taught them. Second, He fed them. He met their spiritual and physical needs.

        b. He took what little he had available, blessed it, and multiplied it. "And they did all eat, and were filled" (Mark 6:42). He fed 5,000 men with five loaves and two fishes.

        c. We can be like Jesus and do something about what we see, or we can look the other way, and ignore the need.

    2. Each woman should give what she has, whether much or little, and let Jesus bless and multiply it to feed many people. The little boy gave *all* his lunch. We should likewise, empty out everything for the cause of Christ.

Our sacrifice becomes the source of God's blessing, just as the little boy's lunch was the source God used to bless thousands.

B. What is Sacrifice?

    1. A sacrifice is anything consecrated and offered to God. It is the surrender of some desirable thing on behalf of a higher object, or devotion of it to a claim deemed more pressing.

    2. "In this world it is not what we take up, but what we give up, that makes us rich."
                                   Henry Ward Beecher

    3. Jesus said in Luke 9:23-29. "If any man will come after me, let him deny himself, and take up his cross daily, and follow me. For whosoever will save his life shall lose it: but whosoever will lose his life for my sake, the same shall save it."

    4. Sacrifice is surrender of selfish desires for higher purposes. It is dying to self.

        a. "He must give up all right to himself."
                                J.B. Phillips

        b. "For whoever chooses to save his lower life will lose his higher life"
                                Charles B. Williams

            i. Paul testified in I Corinthians 15:31, "I die daily."

            ii. I Corinthians 9:27 says, "I keep my body under subjection."

iii. "But I keep on beating and bruising my body and making it my slave."
Charles B. Williams

iv This does not mean that you physically beat your body, but that your carnal will and desires of the flesh are kept under subjection to the higher will of God.

C. As Jesus lived a sacrificial life, so must we.

1. Romans 12:1 says, "I beseech you therefore, brethren, by the mercies of God, that ye present your bodies a living sacrifice, holy, acceptable unto God, which is your reasonable service."

2. The following is Romans 12:1 divided into segments with translations.

a. *"I beseech you"*
"I appeal to you ... and beg of you"
The Amplified New Testament

b. *"by the mercies of God"*
"Because of God's compassion"
Olaf M. Norlie

c. *"that ye present your bodies a living sacrifice"*
"to offer your very selves to him: a living sacrifice."
W.J. Coreybeare

"to make a decisive dedication of your bodies as a living sacrifice."
Charles B. Williams

3. "God Counted Crosses"
I counted dollars while God counted crosses,
I counted gains while He counted losses,

I counted by worth by the things gained in store
But He sized me up by the scars that I bore.
I coveted honors and sought for degrees,
He wept as He counted the hours on my knees;
I never knew until one day by the grave
How vain are the things that we spend life to save;
I did not yet know until my loved one went above
That richest is he who is rich in God's love.

The Brethren Evangelist

4.   Philippians 2:5 says, "Let this mind be in you, which was also in Christ Jesus." What kind of a mind was Paul referring to? The answer is in Philippians 2:7-8.

   a.   Verse 7 says, "But made himself of no reputation, and took upon him the form of a servant."

   b.   Verse 8 says, "He humbled himself, and became obedient unto death, even the death of the cross."

      i.   *"Emptied Himself"*
            The American Standard Version

      ii.   *"And took upon Him the form of a slave"*
            W.J. Corybeare

      iii.   *"And lived obediently to the extreme of death"*
            The Berkeley Version of the New Testament

5.   David Livingstone made a few statements that every woman who is a follower of Christ should keep posted on her mirror. He wrote the following: "People talk of the sacrifice I have made in spending so much of my life in Africa.
   "Can that be called a sacrifice which is simply paid back as small part of the great debt owing to our God, which we can never repay? Is that a sacrifice which

brings its own reward of healthful activity, the consciousness of doing good, peace of mind, and a bright hope of a glorious hereafter?

"Away with such a word, such a view, and such a thought! It is emphatically no sacrifice. Say rather it is a privilege. Anxiety, sickness, suffering or danger now and then, with a foregoing of the common conveniences and charities of this life, may make us pause and cause the spirit to waver and sink; but let this only be for us. I never made a sacrifice. Of this we ought not to talk when we remember the great sacrifice which He made who left His Father's throne on high to give Himself for us."

6. "The cedar tree is a wonderful type of the Christian. It grows by dying. As it develops, stately and beautiful, putting forth new boughs and leaves, the old ones drop off to give strength to the new ones. Likewise the saints live to die and die to live."

                                        Vernon Hart

7. The above quote means that your carnal will and desires of the flesh are kept under subjection to the higher will of God. This is done through prayer, fasting, devouring the Word of God, the strength of the human will, and the power of the Holy Spirit.

D. Although these five components are Bible studies by themselves, the following scriptures will portray the importance of them.

1. *Prayer*: See the following Scriptures:

    •   Luke 18:1 says, "Men ought always to pray, and not to faint."

    •   Jude 1:20 says, "But ye beloved building up yourselves on your must holy faith, praying in the Holy Ghost."

2.   *Fasting*: Fasting helps break the flesh barrier. For more
     information on this read my book, *When Ye Fast*.
     Jesus was instructing his followers in Matthew
     Chapter 6 to lay up treasures in heaven and to seek
     the things of God. He had just talked about the three
     basic foundations for Christian living: prayer, giving, and
     fasting (Matthew 6:3, 5-15, 16-18). See the following
     Scriptures:

     - Philippians 2:8 says, "And being found in fashion
       as a man, he humbled himself, and became obedient
       unto death." **How did Jesus humble Himself as a
       man? He fasted and prayed**.

     - Matthew 4:2 says, "And when he had fasted forty
       days and forty nights, he was afterward an
       hungred."

     - Matthew 26:36 says, "Then cometh Jesus with
       them unto a place called Gethsemane, and saith
       unto the disciples, Sit ye here, while I go and pray
       yonder." (He was preparing for what was to
       come.)

     - Matthew 26:38 says, "O my Father, if it be
       possible, let this cup pass from me: nevertheless not
       as I will, but as thou wilt."(The will of the flesh
       became subject to the will of God.)

3.   *Devouring the word of God*: See the following
     Scriptures:

     - Psalm 119:105 says, "Thy word is a lamp unto my
       feet, and a light unto my path."

     - Psalm 119:11 says, "Thy word have I hid in
       mine heart, that I might not sin against thee."

- Hebrews 4:12 says, "For the word of God is quick, and powerful."

- Colossians 3:16 says, "Let the word of Christ dwell in you richly."

4. *The human will*: See the following Scriptures:

- Paul indicates that it is possible for a person to have power over their own will in I Corinthians 7:37, "He that standeth steadfast in his heart... but hath power over his own will."

- Proverbs 16:32 says, "He that is slow to anger is better than the mighty; and he that ruleth his spirit than he that taketh a city."

5. *Holy Spirit*: See the following Scriptures:

- Zechariah 4:6 says, "Not by might, nor by power, but by my Spirit, saith the Lord."

- Romans 8:11 says, "But if the Spirit of him that raised up Jesus from the dead dwell in you, he that raised up Christ from the dead shall also quicken your mortal bodies by his Spirit that dwelleth in you."

- Romans 8:13, "For if ye live after the flesh, ye shall die: but if ye *through the Spirit*, do mortify the deeds of the body, ye shall live."

Lesson IV Quiz

1.   What is sacrifice?

2.   Paul speaks about dying daily. What five things can a woman do to help bring her body under subjection or her fleshly will to the higher will of God? Give Scriptural answers.

      a.

      b.

      c.

      d.

      e.

3.   How did Jesus become willing to die on a cross?

Women Who Invest

Lesson V

V. WOMEN WHO INVEST

A. Women of compassion invest in God's kingdom.

    1. Jesus told a story about a rich man who wanted to tear down his barns. Then he spoke to his soul and said, "Soul, thou hast much goods laid up for many years; take thine ease, eat, drink, and be merry." (Luke 12:19).

        a. What was God's response to this self-centered outlook? "But God said into him, Thou fool, this night thy soul shall be required of thee: then whose shall those things be, which thou hast provided? So is he that layeth up treasures for himself, and is not rich toward God" (Luke 12:20-21).

        b. Jesus went on to instruct them, "But rather seek ye the kingdom of God; and all these things shall be added to you." (Luke 12:31).

        c. The gist of the story is this: anyone who does not seek the things of God and lay up treasures in heaven is considered a fool by God.

    2. Jesus likens the kingdom of heaven to a man traveling to a far country, who called three servants, and gave them each talents. The first two men increased what the man had given them, but the third man hid his. When the Lord

of the manor returned, he asked for an accounting of what they had done with what he had given them. The first two received a blessing from him because they had invested their money. "Well done, thou hast been faithful over a few things, I will make thee a ruler over many things" (Matthew 25:21).

a. Two basic principles are proven here:

  i. Investment is rewarded by God.

  ii. Investment multiplies.

b. The other side of the coin reflects that poor stewardship or doing nothing with what one has, is not only frowned upon by the Lord, but is scathingly rebuked and punished.

  i. He said, "Thou wicked and slothful servant,...take therefore the talent from him, and give it unto him which hath ten talents. And cast ye the unprofitable servant into outer darkness" (Matthew 25:26,28,30).

  ii. This proves that those who do not bring profit to the kingdom of God, because they do nothing, are considered wicked and slothful.

3. The root word of compassion is compass.

a. According to Webster's Dictionary the verb form of compass means to purpose, to reach, to obtain, to bring about, or to accomplish.

  i. Paul mentioned his purpose in II Timothy 3:10. "Thou hast fully known my doctrine, manner of life, purpose."

ii. What was his purpose? Paul's world was wrapped up in Jesus Christ and His purpose. "For I determined not to know anything among you, save Jesus Christ, and him crucified" (I Corinthians 9:23).

iii. He also said, "For though I be free from all men, yet have I made myself servant unto all, that I might gain more" (I Corinthians 9:19). "I do this for the gospel's sake" (I Corinthians 9:23).

iv. Paul was investing in God's kingdom so he might gain, but it was compassion that prompted it. Paul was weeping (v.18) as he spoke these words. "I count all things but loss for the excellency of the knowledge of Christ Jesus my Lord: for whom I have suffered the loss of all things, and do count them but dung, that I may win Christ" (Philippians 3:8).

v. He lost all things that men count as important in order to invest in God's kingdom. His investment cost him everything.

b. We have to admire General Booth's words he spoke after receiving news he was losing his sight. This eighty year old man addressed an audience of over 4,000 in London. He said, "I want to do more for humanity, and I want to do a great deal for Jesus. There are thousands of poor, wretched, suffering and sinning people crying out to us for help, and I want to do something for them."

c. The challenge to every Christian woman is to re-evaluate her purpose in life, and see if it is wrapped up in doing a great deal more for Jesus.

B.   It is important to be rich in God.

    1.   In Luke 12:21, Jesus is speaking about the man who was only rich in worldly goods and how foolish he was because he was, "not rich toward God." This was a parable.

    2.   In Luke 16 Jesus tells a story that concerns real people. It is not a parable.

        a.   Verse 19 says, "There was a certain rich man, which was clothed in purple and fine linen, and fared sumptuously every day:

        b.   Verse 20 says, "And there was a certain beggar named Lazarus, which was laid at his gate, full of sores."

        c.   Verse 21 says, "And desiring to be fed with the crumbs which fell from the rich man's table: moreover the dogs came and licked his sores."

        d.   Verse 22 says, "And it came to pass, that the beggar died, and was carried by the angels into Abraham's bosom: the rich man also died, and was buried."

        e.   Verse 23 says, " And in hell he lift up his eyes, being in torments, and seeth Abraham afar off, and Lazarus in his bosom."

    3.   Why did the rich man go to hell? Because he was rich only in earthly goods, but not rich in God.

        a.   He refused to help the beggar named Lazarus.

        b.   There is a curse on those who do not obey the second commandment.

i. When they did not feed the poor, visit the prisoners, clothe the naked, or visit the sick, Jesus said, "In as much as ye did it not to one on the least of these, ye did it not to me. And these shall go away into everlasting punishment" (Matthew 10:45-46).

ii. "He that oppresseth the poor reproacheth his maker (Proverbs 14:31). "He that despiseth his neighbour sinneth" (Proverbs 14:21).

4. Who is our neighbor?

a. Jesus answers this in the story of the good Samaritan. A man was robbed, beaten and left for dead by the side of the road. A priest passed him by, and so did a Levite. But then a man with *compassion* entered the picture.

i. Luke 10:33 says, "But a certain Samaritan and when he saw him, he had compassion on him."

ii. Verse 34 says, "And went to him, and bound up his wounds, pouring in oil and wine, and set him on his own beast, and brought him to an inn, and took care of him."

iii. Verse 35 says, "And on the morrow when he departed, he took out two pence, and gave them to the host, and said unto him, Take care of him; and whatsoever thou spendest more, when I come again, I will repay thee."

iv. Verse 36 says, "Which now of these three, thinkest thou, was neighbour unto him that fell among the thieves?"

b.   Notice what the good Samaritan did.

         i.   He bound up his wounds.
         ii.   He poured in oil and wine.
         iii.   He set him on his own beast.
         iv.   He brought him to an inn.
         v.   He took care of him.
         vi.   He paid for his lodging and care at the inn out of his own pocket.

c.   Jesus clinched the story by saying, "Go, and do thou likewise" (Luke 6:37). This story was told in answer to the question asked after Jesus told them to love thy neighbor as thyself. The question was, "Who is my neighbor?" (Luke 6:29).

d.   This story indicates that anyone who has a need is our neighbor, and we sin if we do not help them in whatever way we can.

Lesson V Quiz

1. What was God's response to the self-centered outlook of the rich man? Give Scriptural answer.

2. What two basic principles are proven in the story of the talents?

   a.

   b.

3. What is the root word of compassion and what does it mean?

4. Why is it important to be rich towards God?

5. Who is our neighbor?

6. What six things did the good Samaritan do for the wounded man?

   a.
   b.
   c.
   d.
   e.
   f.

7. What did Jesus tell us to do at the end of the story of the good Samaritan?

Women Who
Triumph Over
Hell

Lesson VI

VI. WOMEN WHO TRIUMPH OVER HELL

A.   The cry of heaven is, "save the lost."

1.   Jude 1:21,22 says, "And some have compassion, making a difference: And others save with fear, pulling them out of the fire; hating even the garment spotted by the flesh."

    a.   The following are translations of these verses:

        i.   *"Flesh referred to is the whole natural or unregenerate man, spirit, soul and body, as centered upon self, prone to sin, and opposed to God."*
C.I. Scofield, D.D.

        ii.   *"And save some, snatching them out of the fire."*
The American Standard version.

        iii.   *"The very clothing that is contaminated with sensuality."*
The New English Bible.

        iv.   *"While you hate even the garment stained by the flesh."*
Richard Frances Weymouth.

b. Heaven's cry is not only, "save the lost," but there is a reward for those that do. Daniel 12:3 says, "And they that be wise shall shine as the brightness of the firmament; and they that turn many to righteousness as the stars for ever and ever."

2. How can a woman snatch or pull people from the flames of hell?

   a. She can pray for people.

      i. Jesus prayed for Peter. Luke 22:31-32 says, "And the Lord said, Simon, Simon, behold Satan hath desired to have you, that he may sift you as wheat: But I have prayed for thee, that thy faith fail not."

      ii. Paul prayed for many people.

         • Colossians 1:2-3 says, "to the saints and faithful brethren in Christ which are at Colosse: Grace be unto you . . . We give thanks to God and the Father of our Lord Jesus Christ, **praying always** for you

         • I Thessalonions 3:10 says, "Night and day praying exceedingly that we might see your face, and might perfect that which is lacking in your faith."

      iii. The widows specifically were instructed to pray.
         • I Timothy 5:5, "Now that she is a widow indeed, and desolate, trusteth in God, and continueth in supplications and prayers night and day."

- Edgar J. Goodspeed translates it like this: "And devotes herself to prayers and entreaties." This is exemplified by Anna in the book of Luke.

- Luke 2:36-37 says, "And there was one Anna, a prophetess, . . . And she was a widow of about four-score and four years, which departed not from the temple, but served God with fastings and prayers night and day."

b. Not only must you pray, but you must also fast for people.

    i. Jesus said some spirits can only be broken by fasting and prayer combined. He is the authority on this, because He accomplished a 40 day fast at the beginning of His ministry. Mark 9:29 says, "This kind can come forth by nothing, but by prayer and fasting." These words were spoken by Jesus after the disciples could not cast the dumb spirit out of a boy. The spirit tore him and caused him to fall on the ground foaming at the mouth. This spirit would have caused the boy to cast himself into the fire, and destroy himself.

    ii. Prayer and fasting unto God places a person into another dimension. As the desires of the flesh are subdued, and a hunger after the Spirit is pursued, something happens in the spirit realm. New faith is released, and as the person decreases in satisfying the carnal woman, the spirit woman is increased.

c. Invite people to come to church where they will hear the gospel preached and feel the converting power of the Lord.

    i. God desires that churches be full. Luke 14:23 says, "And the Lord said unto the Servant, go out into the highways and hedges, and compel them to come in, that my house may be filled."

    ii. Do not be choosey; ask everybody. Luke 14:21 says "Go out quickly into the streets and lanes of the cities and bring in hither the poor, and the maimed, and the halt, and the blind."

    iii. Much of the ministry of Jesus was spent with people. He went to where they were.

    iv. The church must go to where the people are, and give them the message of deliverance.

d. Make an effort to teach them the word of God.

    i. When Apollos, an eloquent man and mighty in the scriptures, was preaching in the synagogue, Priscilla and Aquilla heard him. They realized he was only partially enlightened.

    ii. They had two choices. Leave him alone, go on their way or talk to him more about God. Acts 18:25 says, "This man was instructed in the way of the Lord; and being fervent in the spirit, he spake and taught diligently the things of the Lord, knowing only the baptism of John."

  iii. Priscilla and Aquilla made the right decision. Acts 18:26 says, "And he began to speak boldly in the synagogue: whom when Aquilla and Priscilla had heard, they took him unto them, and expounded unto him the way of God more perfectly."

  iv. Their decision resulted in Apollos receiving the Holy Ghost and becoming a worker in the early church along with Paul. See Acts 18:27-28; Acts 19:1-6; I Cor. 1:12; I Cor. 3:4-6.

 e. Minister to people in prayer and with power.

  i. To pray *for* people is necessary, but it is also important to pray *with* people. Pray until the victory comes.

  ii. Help them pull down strong-holds, bind spirits and be set free.

  iii. You are anointed by God, and filled with His spirit to witness and help others find deliverance.
Recently during a women's prayer meeting, we witnessed to a woman who was bound by unclean spirits. She threw herself on the floor, and we commanded the unclean spirits to come out of her in the name of Jesus. She stopped rolling around and begin to speak with other tongues as a spirit of peace transformed her features. The Holy Ghost power is the same for men and women.

B. Remember that God stands behind you in your efforts.

1. The Spirit helps you pray.

a. Romans 8:26 says, "The spirit also helpeth our infirmities: for we know not what we should pray for as we ought: but the spirit itself maketh intercession for us with groanings which cannot be uttered."

b. Ephesians 6:18 says, "Praying always with all prayer and supplications in the Spirit." The armor is a gift from God with which we are equipped. Prayer is also a gift from God. There would be no praying in the Spirit, if there was not a God who provided it.

2. We are promised that the gates of hell shall not prevail against the Church (Matthew 16:18). This means hell will be a failure in its efforts against the Church, *if* the Church holds out until victory comes.

   a. Prevail means to predominate, overcome, succeed, or triumph. The antonym is failure.

   b. Romans 8:31 says, "What shall we then say to these things? If God be for us, who can be against us?"

   c. Romans 8:37 says, "Nay in all these things we are more than conquerors through him that loved us."

   d. I John 4:4 says, "Ye are of God, little children, and have overcome them: because greater is he that *is in you*, than he that is in the world."

3. The spirit enlightens your understanding.

   a. Read Ephesians 1:17-19.

        i.   Verse 17 says, "That the God of our Lord Jesus Christ, the Father of glory, may give unto you the spirit of wisdom and revelation in the knowledge of him."

        ii.   Verse 18 says, "The eyes of your understanding being enlightened; that ye may know what is the hope of his calling, and what the riches of the glory of his inheritance in the saints."

        iii.   Verse 19 says, "And what is the exceeding greatness of his power to usward who believe, according to the working of his mighty power."

b.   The following are translations of Ephesians 1:17-18.

        i.   *"That you may receive that inner illumination of the spirit."*
                JB Phillips

        ii.   *"And that the eyes of your heart may be flooded with light."*
                Helen Bartlett Montgomery.

4.   God not only stands behind you and supports you, but He also will judge you according to your efforts.

a.   Read II Corinthians 5:9-10.

        i.   Verse 9 says, "Wherefore we labour, that, whether present or absent, we may be accepted of him."

        ii.   Verse 10 says, "For we must all appear before the judgment seat of Christ; that every one may receive the things done in his body, according to that he hath done, whether it be good or bad."

        iii.   Verse 11 says, "Knowing therefore the terror of the Lord, we persuade men."

    b.   Paul not only gave another reason why he worked to persuade men toward the gospel of Jesus Christ, but he stated his motive. This should be our motive.
II Corinthians 5:14 says, "for the love of Christ constraineth us."

5.   Remember, it will be worth it!

    a.   I Corinthians 2:9 says, "Eye hath not seen, nor ear heard, neither have entered into the heart of Man, the things which God hath prepared from them that love him."

        i.   How do we know if we can partake of the promises in I Corinthians 2:9? Jesus said, "If ye love me, keep my commandments" (John 14:15).

        ii.   Jesus said also, "My mother and my brethren are these which hear the word of God, and do it" (Luke 8:21).

        iii.   See Matthew 12:48-50 and Mark 3:33-35.

    b.   In addressing the church of Philadelphia (which means brotherly love), Jesus said, "Him that overcometh will I make a pillar in the temple of my God, and he shall go no more out: and I will write upon him the name of my God . . and I will write upon him my new name." (Revelation 3:12).

Lesson VI Quiz

1. What is the cry of heaven?

2. What does Jude 1:21-22 instruct the Christian to do?

3. How can a woman snatch or pull people from hell?

   a.

   b.

   c.

   d.

   e.

4. How does God help her?

   a.

   b.

   c.

   d.

5. What does Revelation promise the overcomer?

*Women of
Courage Who
Care*

Lesson VII

VII. WOMEN OF COURAGE WHO CARE

A.   Birthing a soul, or bringing a soul into the full stature of Christ, is not always easy. This takes work and courage.

    1.   What is courage?

        a.   Courage is bravery, valor, resoluteness, boldness. It is having a daring spirit, or a defiance of danger and determination during hardship.

        b.   Courage is defying the odds, looking difficulty in the face without flinching, and showing fortitude in the fire.

    2.   This tenacity and fortitude is felt in Paul's statement in Galatians 4:19, "My little children, of whom I travail in birth again until Christ be formed in you."

        a.   He was saying, " I am not letting go. I am travailing again. I am praying until!"

        b.   Paul refused to give up, he had the courage to care.

3.   I read a story that could be told by many. Thousands of teachers will identify with the following story which shows that things are not always as they seem on the surface. Winning souls and caring must dig deeper than the surface.

A young man was asked to teach a Sunday School class of junior high boys. There was one boy that was so bad that nobody wanted to teach him. The boy literally tore the class apart and after having tried everything, the teacher went to the Superintendent and told him he was quitting. The Superintendent said, "Before you quit, promise me you will visit his home." The young man agreed to do so, and went looking for the student's home. It was a little shack at the end of a long, dusty lane. When he knocked at the door a woman answered and said, "Yeah, so what do you want?"

When the teacher told the mother who he was, she was very embarrassed and invited the teacher into the house. There he saw a human form lying over by the baseboard who was dead drunk. This was the father of his student. The teacher then realized that the terror of the class was looking for love. In a moment of inspiration, he said, "Son, if I came early next week, will you be there early?" He promised that he would, and the janitor said when he came at 7:00 a.m. the following Sunday, the young boy was sitting on the front steps waiting for his Sunday School teacher to come.

He won that boy to Jesus Christ, simply because he cared enough to go beyond the conventional classroom and probe a little deeper into the needs of a very hurting young boy who had no hope except what he received at Church.

B.   Paul addresses some special women who cared enough to make a difference in the lives of other people. Let us look at some of them. (Romans 16).

1. *Phebe*: Paul writes about her in Romans 16:1-2, "I commend unto you Phebe our sister, which is a servant of the church which is at Cenchrea: That ye receive her in the Lord, as becometh saints, and that ye assist her in whatsoever business she hath need of you: for she hath been a succourer of many, and of myself also."

    a. Dr. Herbert Lockyer says this about her. "That she must have been a woman of some consequence appears from the fact that she planned a long journey to Rome on business of her own, and offered to convey to the saint's there, Paul's letter."

    b. He also writes, "Phoebe was not merely a confessing and active believer, she was also a ministrant of the church. The word for "servant" is *diakonos* from which we have "decon" or "deacones." Phoebe occupied a position in the church where she could be a teacher of all female inquirers of the faith, and be active in the relief of the temporal needs of the poor among the flock. The word Paul used for "succourer," *prostatis*, is a most expressive one. It literally means "one who stands by in case of need." She not only helped Paul himself, but helped many others also."

2. *Priscilla*: Romans 16:3 says, "Greet Priscilla and Aquila my helpers in Christ Jesus." See Acts 18:2,18,26; Romans 16:3; I Corinthians 16:19; II Timothy 4:19

    a. Dr. Herbert Lockyer writes, "Priscilla and her husband were always paired together. Their two hearts beat as one. Harmoniously, they labored together in the service of the church. They walked as one for they had mutually agreed to put Christ first."

77

b. They were humble tent makers who greatly enriched the lives of two of the greatest preachers: Paul and Apollos. Not only did they enrich these two lives, but they cared enough to help many others.

c. Paul gives further insight into their dedication and courage. Romans 16:4-5 says, "Who have for my life laid down their own necks: unto whom not only I give thanks, but also to all the churches of the Gentiles. Likewise greet the church that is in their house."

d. As they were rich in the knowledge of the Scriptures, so they shared it with others. They did not keep it to themselves.

3. *Tryphena and Tryphosa*: Romans 16;12 says, "Salute Tryphena and Tryphosa, who labor in the Lord." Since there were many Christian women, it is an honor for Paul to mention them.

a. Dr. Herbert Lockyer writes, "They must have been conspicuous in the service at the church at Rome, perhaps deaconess's, otherwise Paul would not have singled them out for his expression of gratitude for their devoted labor in the Lord."

b. He also writes, "Early christian inscriptions in cemeteries used chiefly for the servants of the emperor contain both of these female names, and so can be identified as being among, 'the saints of Caesar's household' (Philippians 4:22)."

4. *Mary*: Romans 16:6 says, "Greet Mary, who bestowed much labour on us ."

a.   Not much is known about this Mary of Rome, but she stands for all the women down through the ages who have labored greatly for the cause of Christ.

b.   Paul again speaks about the women who helped him in Philippias 4:3. "And I intreat thee also, true yoke fellow, help those women which labored with me in the gospel, with Clement also, and with other my fellow laborers, whose names are in the book of life."

c.   The following two things are at the top of the list of the greatest things that can be said about a woman.

   i.   "Her name is in the book of Life."

   ii.   "She has labored to help many for the gospel's sake."

Lesson VII Quiz

1.   What is courage?

2.   Name four women who made a difference in the lives of other people. Give Scripture references and what they did.

    a.

    b.

    c.

    d.

3.   What does it take to birth a soul or bring them into the full stature of Christ?

    a.

    b.

4.   What are two of the greatest things that can be said about a woman?

    a.

    b.

Women of the Spirit Bible Study

Lesson VIII

VIII. WOMEN WHO FOLLOW JESUS

A. Women who follow Jesus, minister to Him and to other people.

1. Read Luke 8:1-3

   a. Verse one says, "And it came to pass afterward, that he went through every city and village, preaching and shewing the glad tiding of the kingdom of God: and the twelve were with him."

   b. Verse two says, "And certain women, which had been healed of evil spirits and infirmities, Mary called Magdalene, out of whom went seven devils,"

   c. Verse three says, "And Joanna the wife of Chuza Herod's steward, and Susanna, and many others, which *ministered* unto him of their substance."

2. When Jesus had delivered Joanna and Mary Magdalene of evil spirits and infirmities, they ministered unto him of their substance.

a. Dr. Herbert Lockyer writes of Joanna, "It is evident that this female of the upper class, restored to normal health by Christ, gave her life for Him. She is here seen as one of the traveling company who went before Christ and the twelve to arrange for their hospitable reception. Out of her own resources many expenses were met, and in this way she ministered unto Him of her substance. Having freely received His healing touch, she freely gave of herself and of her means for His welfare."

    i. He also writes, "Chuza the husband of Joanna, was the "steward" of Herod. Chuza must have been a man of intelligence and ability in order to hold the position he did as manager of Herod's income expenditure. As Joanna was known as one of the Lord's disciples, naturally she would speak of Him among Herod's servants. The office of Chuza gave Joanna an excellent opportunity of witnessing in the palace."

    ii. Dr. Lockyer continues, "Tradition has it that Chuza lost his position in Herod's palace because of his wife's conversion to Christianity and her courageous testimony among Herod's servants.

b. Mary Magdalene ministered to Jesus often.

    i. Dr. Herbert Lockyer writes, "Delivered, Mary became a disciple. Freed from Satanic bondage she became harnessed to the chariot of the Lord, and her personal ministrations, along with those of other women who had been healed, greatly aided Jesus in His missionary activities as He went from place to place preaching and teaching His message."

        ii.   Dr. Herbert Lockyer also wrote, "Once Mary was healed and saved, She practiced her faith in following Jesus and ministering to Him and His disciples of her substance. Are there not a thousand ways in which converted and consecrated women can serve the master acceptably... Are we loving and serving Him to the limit of our capacity, daily witnessing to the power of His resurrection?"

3.   Mary of Bethany not only followed Jesus, but she also ministered to Him, and became an evangelist (one that helps spread the gospel of Jesus Christ).

    a.   She chose to learn of Him and sit at his feet. Luke 10:42 says, "But one thing is needful: and Mary hath chosen that good part, which shall not be taken away from her."

    b.   She chose to minister to Him. Read John 12:1-3.

        i.   Verse 1 says, "Then Jesus six days before the Passover came to Bethany, where Lazarus was which had been dead, whom he raised from the dead."

        ii.   Verse 2 says, "There they made him a supper; and Martha served; but Lazarus was one of them that sat at the table with him."

        iii.   Verse 3 says, "Then took Mary a pound of ointment of spikenard very costly, and anointed the feet with her hair: and the house was filled with the odour of the ointment."

c. She chose to tell others about Him. John 11:45 says, "Then many of the Jews which came to Mary, and had seen the things which Jesus did, believed on Him." She was an effective evangelist!

B. Women who follow Jesus are loyal and stay to the end.

1. These women followed Him while He ministered to others, and they were at the cross.

a. Luke 23:49 says, "And all his acquaintance, and the women that followed him from Galilee, stood afar off, beholding these things."

b. Matthew 27:55 says, "And many women were there beholding afar off, which followed Jesus from Galilee, ministering unto him:"

2. They followed Him to the sepulcher.

a. Luke 23:55, "And the women also, which came with him from Galilee, followed after, and beheld the sepulchre, and how his body was laid."

b. Matthew 27:61 says, "And there was Mary Magdalene, and the other Mary, sitting over against the sepulchre."

3. They were still ministering to Him even in His death.

a. Luke 23:56 says, "And they returned, and prepared spices and ointments; and rested the sabbath day according to the commandment."

b. Luke 24:1 says, "How upon the first day of the week, very early in the morning, they came unto the sepulchre, bringing the spices which they had repaired, and certain others with them."

4. They were the first ones who talked to the angel.

    a. Matthew 28:5 says, "And the angel answered and said unto the women, fear not ye: for I know that ye seek Jesus which was crucified."

    b. John 20:11-12 says, "Mary stood... an seeth two angels in white."

    c. Luke 24:4-5 says, "And it came to pass, as they were much perplexed thereabout, behold, two men stood by them in shining garments: And as they were afraid, and bowed down their faces to the earth, they said unto them, Why seek ye the living among the dead?"

5. They were told by the angel to go give a message to the disciples.

    a. Matthew 28:7 says, "Go quickly, and tell his disciples that he is risen from the dead."

    b. Please read Mark 16:5-7.

6. While they were on their way to give the message from the angel, Jesus appeared to them.

    a. Matthew 28:9-10 says, "And as they went to tell his disciples, behold, Jesus met them...Then said Jesus unto them, be not afraid: go tell my brethren."

    b. Matthew 16:9 says, "Now when Jesus was risen early the first day of the week, he appeared first to Mary Magdalene, out of whom he had cast seven devils."

7. The lives that Jesus changed followed this pattern.

    a. They were converted and forgiven.

    b. They ministered to Jesus and others, and gave their all.

    c. They stayed with Him until the end.

8. What were the results?

    a. Their names were written in the Book of Life.

    b. They had an angelic visitation.

    c. Jesus spoke to them personally.

        i. He said, "Be not afraid."

        ii. He also said, "Go and tell."

C. Women who follow Jesus learn to linger near Him.

1. The women who linger and wait will see the glory of the Lord.

    a. The disciples were in a hurry. They arrived, looked around, and left, but the women lingered. They were the ones the angels appeared to.

        i. John 20:3-4,6,10 says, "Peter therefore went forth, and that other disciple, and came to the sepulchre. So they ran both together: and the other disciple did outrun Peter, and came first to the sepulchre. Then cometh Simon Peter following him, and went into the sepulchre... Then the disciples went away again unto their own home."

    ii.   "But Mary stood without at the sepulchre weeping: and as she wept, she stooped down, and looked into the sepulchre. And seeth two angels in white sitting, the one at the head, and the other at the feet, where the body of Jesus had lain." (John 20:11-12).

b.   The disciples went inside, looked around, saw nothing supernatural, and went home, but Mary weeping and brokenhearted lingered. In the same tomb the disciples had just looked, she saw two angels.

2.   Women who linger at his feet choose that which pleases the Lord.

a.   Luke 10:39 says, "And she had a sister called Mary, which also sat at Jesus' feet, and heard his word."

b.   Martha being perturbed at Mary because she lingered too long said, "Lord, dost thou not care that my sister hath left me to serve alone?" (Luke10:40).

c.   Jesus knowing the nature of the two women simply said, "One thing is needful: and Mary hath chosen that good part, which shall not be taken away from her" (Luke 10:42).

d.   No one can take away the precious experiences, which come only from lingering in His presence, ministering to Him, and beholding His glory.

D.   Women who follow Jesus, help win souls.

    1.   Walter B. Knight tells the following story. "An elderly woman was being conducted through a great cathedral in Europe. The guide spoke of its beauty of design, calling special attention to its statues and wonderful paintings. The old lady was unimpressed. At the conclusion of the tour, she asked the guide, 'How many souls have been saved here this year?' ' My dear lady,' said the embarrassed guide, 'this is a cathedral, not a chapel.' "

    2.   May each woman not only seek to be beautiful as a cathedral, but let her also seek to be as a chapel where souls are won.

Lesson VIII Quiz

1. The women who follow Jesus, do three main things. What are they? Please, elaborate.

   a.

   b.

   c.

2. What did Joanna and Mary Magdalene do after Jesus delivered them?

3. What three things did Mary of Bethany choose to do?

   a.

   b.

   c.

4. What were the results of following Jesus?

   a.
   b.
   c.

Women of the Spirit Multi-Volume Bible Study

Volume I: Love, God's Way

Volume II: Faith, Prayer, & Spiritual Warfare

Volume III: All About Trials

Volume IV: Wisdom, Attitudes, Character

Volume V: Women of Compassion

These can be ordered from:

Radiant Life Publications
9025 N. West Lane
Stockton, CA 95210
Ph. 209-469-2210
Fax 209-476-7888